EXPLORING THE STATES

Texas

THE LONE STAR STATE

by Kristin Schuetz

BELLWETHER MEDIA · MINNEAPOLIS, MN

Note to Librarians, Teachers, and Parents:

Blastoff! Readers are carefully developed by literacy experts and combine standards-based content with developmentally appropriate text.

Level 1 provides the most support through repetition of high-frequency words, light text, predictable sentence patterns, and strong visual support.

Level 2 offers early readers a bit more challenge through varied simple sentences, increased text load, and less repetition of high-frequency words.

Level 3 advances early-fluent readers toward fluency through increased text and concept load, less reliance on visuals, longer sentences, and more literary language.

Level 4 builds reading stamina by providing more text per page, increased use of punctuation, greater variation in sentence patterns, and increasingly challenging vocabulary.

Level 5 encourages children to move from "learning to read" to "reading to learn" by providing even more text, varied writing styles, and less familiar topics.

Whichever book is right for your reader, Blastoff! Readers are the perfect books to build confidence and encourage a love of reading that will last a lifetime!

This edition first published in 2014 by Bellwether Media, Inc.

No part of this publication may be reproduced in whole or in part without written permission of the publisher. For information regarding permission, write to Bellwether Media, Inc., Attention: Permissions Department, 5357 Penn Avenue South, Minneapolis, MN 55419.

Library of Congress Cataloging-in-Publication Data

Schuetz, Kristin.
Texas / by Kristin Schuetz.
     pages cm. – (Blastoff! readers. Exploring the states)
Includes bibliographical references and index.
Summary: "Developed by literacy experts for students in grades three through seven, this book introduces young readers to the geography and culture of Texas"– Provided by publisher.
ISBN 978-1-62617-043-8 (hardcover : alk. paper)
1. Texas–Juvenile literature. I. Title.
F386.3.S38 2014
976.4–dc23
                                                                                    2013002649

Printed in the United States of America, North Mankato, MN.

Table of Contents

Where Is Texas?

Texas sits in the south-central part of the United States. It is the second largest state. Texas neighbors New Mexico to the west and Oklahoma to the north. Arkansas and Louisiana touch its eastern border.

In the southwest, the winding Rio Grande separates Texas from Mexico. This river flows east into the **Gulf** of Mexico. The capital city of Austin is in central Texas. It is located within a **megaregion** called the Texas Triangle. The major cities of Dallas-Fort Worth, Houston, and San Antonio form the triangle.

New Mexico

N

W   E

S

Oklahoma

Palo Duro
Canyon State
Park

Arkansas →

Fort Worth ● ● Dallas

Texas

Louisiana →

Austin
★

Houston ●

San Antonio ●

Rio Grande

Gulf of
Mexico

Mexico

History

Spanish explorers first came to Texas in the 1500s. Before that, **Native** Americans lived off the land. Spanish missionaries arrived in the late 1600s to set up **missions**. They tried to **convert** the Native Americans to their Catholic religion. In the 1820s, Mexico ruled Texas. It lost control of the area after the Texas Revolution. Texas joined the United States as the twenty-eighth state in 1845.

Spanish missionaries

Texas Timeline!

1519: Spaniard Alonso Álvarez de Pineda maps the southeastern coast of Texas.

1821: Mexico takes control of Texas.

1835: The Texas Revolution breaks out. Texans fight for independence from Mexico.

1836: Texans lose the Battle of the Alamo to Mexico.

1836: The Republic of Texas is formed.

1845: Texas becomes the twenty-eighth state.

1861-1865: Texas and other southern states fight the North during the Civil War.

1860s-1880s: Cowboys lead cattle drives up north to market.

1901: A large oil field is found on Spindletop Hill.

1963: President John F. Kennedy is shot in Dallas.

2000: Texas Governor George W. Bush is elected the forty-third President of the United States.

Battle of the Alamo

John F. Kennedy

George W. Bush

The Land

Did you know?
Guadalupe Peak is the highest point in Texas. This mountain rises 8,749 feet (2,667 meters) in Big Bend Country.

Many different landscapes fill the large state of Texas. Grassy **plains** stretch across the northern **panhandle** and the southern point of the state. Palm trees in the **subtropical** Rio Grande Valley dot the southernmost tip. Eastern Texas has pine forests and swamps in the north. South of the forests are plains cut by rivers. The rivers make their way to the Gulf Coast.

Big Bend

Texas's Climate
average °F

spring
Low: 56°
High: 78°

summer
Low: 72°
High: 91°

fall
Low: 57°
High: 78°

winter
Low: 38°
High: 61°

Central Texas has **prairies** and rolling hills. Steep **canyons** and rock formations break up the grassy landscape. Dark underground caves are also present. The Guadalupe Mountains, Davis Mountains, and Chisos Mountains elevate western Texas, or Big Bend Country. Desert-like areas also dry out the west.

The Palo Duro Canyon

The Palo Duro Canyon lies in the panhandle near Amarillo, Texas. This huge canyon stretches for 120 miles (193 kilometers) and drops to depths of more than 800 feet (244 meters). The Red River created the canyon. Water **erosion** carved out its unique features.

Special formations define Palo Duro. Lighthouse Peak is by far the most popular. It rises 300 feet (91 meters) to point toward the sky. Multicolored layers make up the sides of the canyon. They show different periods in the earth's history. Many **fossils** have been discovered in the canyon's layers.

Lighthouse Peak

! **fun fact**

Because of its size, many people call Palo Duro the "Grand Canyon of Texas." It is the second largest canyon in the United States.

Wildlife

longhorn

fun fact !

Bluebonnets and other wildflowers add splashes of color to pastures and roadsides. It is a tradition for children to pose for pictures in bluebonnet fields.

Many different animals call Texas home. Several types of rattlesnakes, including the western diamondback, claim territory throughout the state. Only Arizona has more of these **venomous** snakes. Piping plovers, **endangered** whooping cranes, and other birds spend winters along the coast. Mockingbirds treat Texans to beautiful songs all year.

armadillo

Did you know?
The prickly pear cactus is the state plant. It thrives in dry areas of Texas because it can survive droughts.

prickly pear cactus

piping plover

Armadillos and longhorn cattle, the two state mammals, are familiar sights in Texas. The Palo Duro mouse is completely unique to the state. This rodent hides in canyon cracks in the panhandle region. The Guadalupe bass is another rare animal that lives in Texas. It swims in the Guadalupe and other rivers.

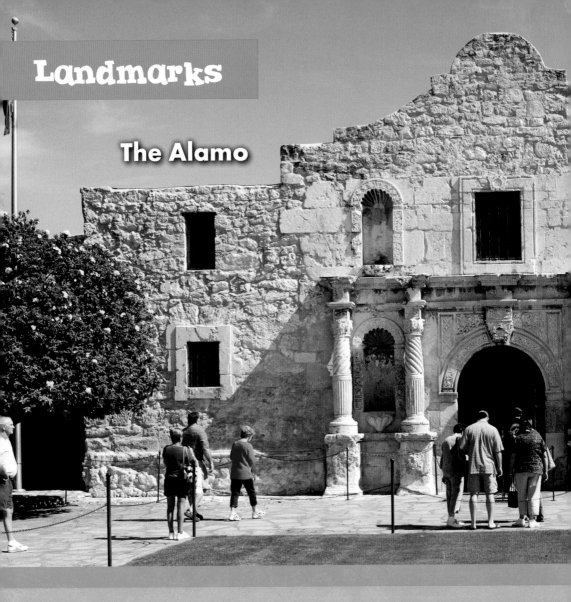

Landmarks

The Alamo

Historical landmarks in Texas cities draw large crowds. The State **Capitol** in Austin is a soft pink color because it is made of granite rock. **Monuments** and statues on the surrounding grounds honor important events and Texans. In San Antonio, the Alamo marks the place where Texans held off the Mexicans for 13 days during the Revolution.

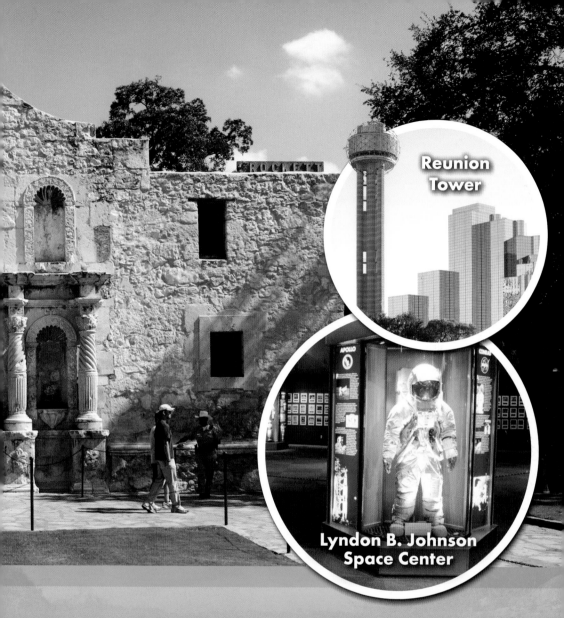

Reunion
Tower

Lyndon B. Johnson
Space Center

Two landmarks in Dallas and Houston have become
popular symbols of their cities. Reunion Tower offers
spectacular views hundreds of feet above Dallas.
Houston's Lyndon B. Johnson Space Center is the site of
NASA's Mission Control Center. This center coordinates
all U.S. flights into space.

San Antonio

San Antonio is the second largest city in Texas. The lively River Walk that follows the San Antonio River is the heart of the city. This series of walkways is lined with lovely restaurants and shops. San Antonians and **tourists** like to stroll along the paths. Some even take boat rides through the **scenic** area.

San Antonio is a city rich in history. San Antonio Missions National Historic Park holds four Spanish missions from the 1700s. The city's most famous mission, the Alamo, lies just north of the other four. Though it was a religious building, it is better known for the battle that took place there. This is just part of San Antonio's long military history. U.S. Army **Fort** Sam Houston has stood in the city since 1876.

Fort Sam Houston

River Walk

Did you know?

Texas generates a lot of wind power. Strong winds in west Texas's wide open spaces spin turbines on wind farms.

Texas is the top producer of oil in the United States. Workers have discovered this **natural resource** in more than half of the state. Farming is another important field of work. Texas farmers raise most of the beef cattle in the nation. They also grow most of the cotton.

Fishers reel in great catches along the Gulf Coast. They snatch shrimp, crabs, oysters, and sea trout from the waters. In major cities, many Texans have **service jobs**. They help the millions of tourists that visit each year.

oil drilling

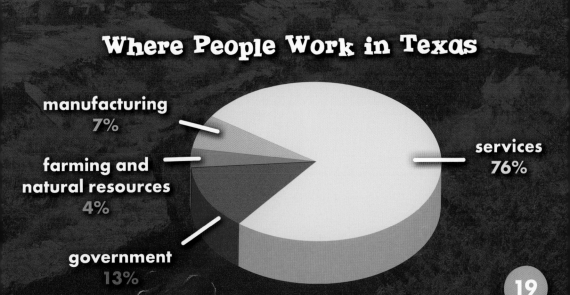

Where People Work in Texas

manufacturing
7%

farming and
natural resources
4%

government
13%

services
76%

Playing

Sports fans have a lot to root for in Texas. For many, nothing is more important than football. From high school games to the NFL, fans are always cheering for their team. Texans are also crazy for **rodeos**. In rodeos, cowboys and cowgirls compete in horse and bull riding events.

Texas is a paradise for people who love the outdoors. Hikers and campers head to the state's many beautiful parks. Beaches along the Gulf Coast are popular places to fish and relax. These sandy shores are also places to hunt for more than 400 different types of seashells.

Dallas Cowboys football

Did you know?

Texans enjoy listening to music in their free time. *Tejano*, a unique blend of American, Mexican, and European styles, was created in the state.

Nachos

Ingredients:

2 cups tortilla chips

1 1/2 cups refried beans

1 1/2 cups cheddar cheese, grated

2 pickled jalapeño peppers, sliced

Salsa

Guacamole

Sour cream

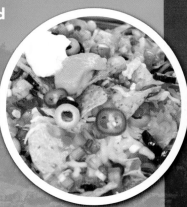

Directions:

1. Preheat the oven to 350°F.

2. Arrange a layer of tortilla chips along the bottom of a wide, shallow baking pan. The layer of tortilla chips can be several chips thick.

3. Spread refried beans over the chips. Sprinkle cheese and jalapeño peppers on top.

4. Bake for 10 minutes, or until cheese is melted.

5. Serve hot with salsa, sour cream, and guacamole.

chili

sopapillas

Texas food is full of flavor and spice. Chili is a popular dish in this state. Most recipes are filled with a lot of meat and hot, spicy chili peppers. Texans also like to use chili in other recipes and on top of hot dogs. Texas is well known for its barbecue. Beef, ribs, and other meats are covered in a smoky, spicy sauce.

! fun fact

Nachos are a classic Tex-Mex snack first made on the Texas-Mexican border. The name comes from the original chef, Ignacio "Nacho" Anaya.

Tex-Mex is a type of food commonly found in the state. It combines American ingredients with Mexican food. Puffy *sopapillas* are one Mexican dessert Texans enjoy. People in the state also love a Czech sweet roll called *kolache*.

Festivals

Texans like to celebrate their state and culture with many festivals. One of the most popular events is the State Fair. It lasts almost a whole month! People enjoy fried foods and the yearly Texas-Oklahoma football game.

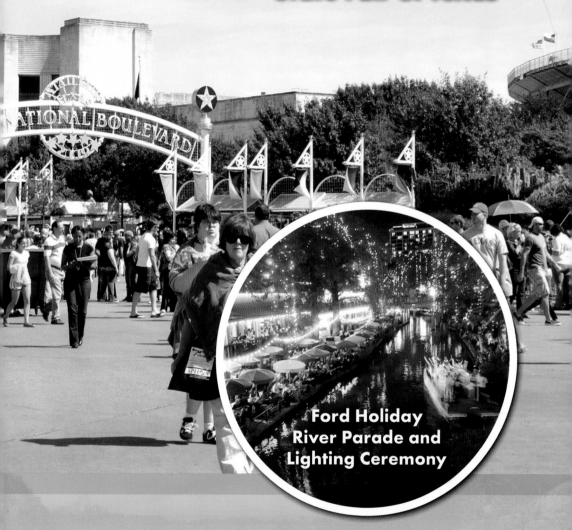

NATIONAL BOULEVARD

Ford Holiday River Parade and Lighting Ceremony

San Antonio hosts the Ford Holiday River Parade and Lighting Ceremony in November. This colorful parade is full of lighted, decorated boats that float down the San Antonio River. Another unique event is the Great Texas Mosquito Festival. At this three-day gathering in Clute, Texans compete in a mosquito calling contest and other fun events.

Cowboys

When people think of Texas, cowboys usually come to mind. Texans quickly adopted the cowboy way of life from the Mexican *vaqueros*. From the 1860s to 1880s, cowboys led longhorns up north on cattle drives to be sold at markets. The cowboys would sing to keep the cattle calm. After a long day of work, cowboys would gather around campfires to tell rhyming stories. This cowboy poetry described their daily life.

Today's cowboys demonstrate their **mastery** of difficult skills at Texas rodeos. They also work on ranches in the state. The King Ranch in Kingsville is one of the biggest in the world. It shows that the cowboy way of life continues to be an important part of the history and culture of Texas.

fun fact

Big Tex, a 52-foot (16-meter) statue of a cowboy, became the main symbol of the State Fair in 1952. Sadly, a fire destroyed the statue in 2012. A brand new one was built for the 2013 State Fair.

Fast Facts About Texas

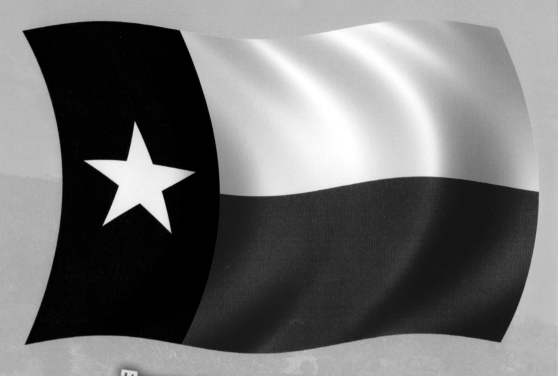

Texas's Flag

The Texas flag is red, white, and blue and features a star. The blue stripe stands for loyalty. The white stripe is for freedom, and the red stripe is for bravery. The lone star is a symbol of unity and independence.

State Bird
northern mockingbird

State Flower
bluebonnet

State Nickname:	The Lone Star State
State Motto:	"Friendship"
Year of Statehood:	1845
Capital City:	Austin
Other Major Cities:	Houston, San Antonio, Dallas, Fort Worth
Population:	25,145,561 (2010)
Area:	266,833 square miles (691,094 square kilometers); Texas is the 2nd largest state.
Major Industries:	oil and natural gas, farming, services
Natural Resources:	oil, natural gas, lumber, limestone, salt, sulfur
State Government:	150 representatives; 31 senators
Federal Government:	36 representatives; 2 senators
Electoral Votes:	38

State Animals
nine-banded armadillo, longhorn

Glossary

canyons—narrow river valleys with steep, tall sides

capitol—the building in which state representatives and senators meet

convert—to change someone's views and beliefs

endangered—at risk of becoming extinct

erosion—the wearing away of land features due to wind or water

fort—a strong building made to protect lands; forts are often occupied by troops and surrounded by other defenses.

fossils—the remains of plants and animals from the past that are preserved in rock

gulf—part of an ocean or sea that extends into land

mastery—expert skill or knowledge

megaregion—a large area packed with major cities

missions—buildings used for religious work

monuments—structures that people build to remember important events or people

native—originally from a specific place

natural resource—a material in the earth that is taken out and used to make products or fuel

panhandle—a narrow stretch of land attached to a larger piece of land

plains—large areas of flat land

prairies—large areas of level or rolling grassland

rodeos—events where people compete at tasks such as bull riding and calf roping; cowboys once completed these tasks as part of their daily work.

scenic—providing beautiful views of the natural surroundings

service jobs—jobs that perform tasks for people or businesses

subtropical—bordering on the tropics; the tropics is a hot, rainy region near the equator.

tourists—people who travel to visit another place

venomous—producing a poison that can harm or kill

To Learn More

AT THE LIBRARY
Coleman, Wim, and Pat Perrin. *The Alamo*. Berkeley Heights, N.J.: MyReportLinks.com Books, 2005.

Harrison, David L. *Cowboys: Voices in the Western Wind*. Honesdale, Penn.: Wordsong, 2012.

Wade, Mary Dodson. *All Around Texas: Regions and Resources*. Chicago, Ill.: Heinemann Library, 2008.

ON THE WEB
Learning more about Texas is as easy as 1, 2, 3.

1. Go to www.factsurfer.com.

2. Enter "Texas" into the search box.

3. Click the "Surf" button and you will see a list of related Web sites.

With factsurfer.com, finding more information is just a click away.

Index

The images in this book are reproduced through the courtesy of: Nordic Photos/ SuperStock, front cover (bottom); Getty Images, pp. 6, 7 (left); (Collection)/ Prints & Photographs Division/ Library of Congress, p. 7 (middle, right); Zack Frank, pp. 8-9, 10-11; Mikenorton, p. 10; Steve Schlaeger, pp. 12-13; Arto Hakola, p. 13 (top); Steve Byland, p. 13 (middle); You Touch Pix of EuToch, p. 13 (bottom); Fred LaBounty, pp. 14-15; Natalia Bratslavsky, p. 15 (top); Richard Cummins/ Glow Images, p. 15 (bottom); Choicegraphx, p. 16 (top); Nik Wheeler/ Alamy, p. 16 (bottom); Dszc, pp. 16-17; Ssucsy, p. 18; Keith Wood/ Corbis/ Glow Images, p. 19; Ken Durden, p. 20; Juanmonino/ Getty Images, pp. 20-21; Pilipphoto, p. 22; Igor Dutina, p. 23 (top); TheCrimsonMonkey, p. 23 (bottom); Q-Images/ Alamy, pp. 24-25; Zuma Press, Inc./ Alamy, p. 25; Dorti, p. 26; JeanneHatch, pp. 26-27; Pakmor, p. 28 (top); Steve Byland, p. 28 (bottom left); Warren Price Photography, p. 28 (bottom right); Imagebroker.net/ SuperStock, p. 29 (left); Tammy Venable, p. 29 (right).